Desert Experiments

11 Science Experiments in One Hour or Less

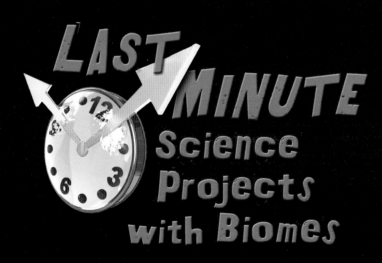

Last Minute Science Projects with Biomes

ROBERT GARDNER

ILLUSTRATED BY TOM LABAFF

Enslow Publishers, Inc.
40 Industrial Road
Box 398
Berkeley Heights, NJ 07922
USA

http://www.enslow.com

Library of Congress Cataloging-in-Publication Data

Gardner, Robert, 1929–

Desert experiments : 11 science experiments in one hour or less / Robert Gardner.

p. cm. — (Last minute science projects with biomes)

Summary: "A variety of science projects that can be done in under an hour, plus a few that take longer for interested students"— Provided by publisher.

Includes index.

ISBN 978-0-7660-5917-7

1. Desert ecology—Experiments—Juvenile literature. 2. Desert biology—Experiments—Juvenile literature. 3. Science projects—Juvenile literature. I. Title.

QH541.5.D4G37 2015

577.54'078—dc23

2013008773

Future editions:

Paperback ISBN: 978-0-7660-5918-4

ePUB ISBN: 978-0-7660-5919-1

Single-User PDF ISBN: 978-0-7660-5920-7

Multi-User PDF ISBN: 978-0-7660-5921-4

Printed in the United States of America

052014 Lake Book Manufacturing, Inc., Melrose Park, IL

10 9 8 7 6 5 4 3 2 1

To Our Readers: We have done our best to make sure all Internet Addresses in this book were active and appropriate when we went to press. However, the author and the publisher have no control over and assume no liability for the material available on those Internet sites or on other Web sites they may link to. Any comments or suggestions can be sent by e-mail to comments@enslow.com or to the address on the back cover.

♻ Enslow Publishers, Inc., is committed to printing our books on recycled paper. The paper in every book contains 10% to 30% post-consumer waste (PCW). The cover board on the outside of each book contains 100% PCW. Our goal is to do our part to help young people and the environment too!

Illustration Credits: Tom LaBaff

Photo Credits: ©1999 Artville, LLC, p. 13; ©Michael Durham/Minden Pictures, p. 34; Shutterstock.com: ©agap, p. 6; ©AZP Worldwide, p. 19 (left); ©AMA, p. 21; ©Max Allen, p. 25; ©You Touch Pix of EuToch, p. 31; ©Lubava, p. 39; ©Lowe R. Llaguno, p. 43; ©Thinkstock: Pascal RATEAU/iStock, p. 5; Jupiterimages/Photos.com, p. 26

Cover Credits: Shutterstock.com: ©Jose Gil (pie plate); ©SmileStudio (wooden ruler); ©R. Gino Santa Maria (laboratory glassware); ©Videowokart (Aeonium—hair); ©bogdan ionescu(cactus—hand); ©Videowokart(agave plant); ©Onur YILDIRIM (clock with yellow arrows)

Contents

LAST MINUTE Science Projects with Biomes

🎗 Contains ideas for more science fair projects.

Are You Running Late?

Do you have a science project that is due soon? If so, this book will help you! Not only does it have experiments about desert biomes, but many of the experiments can be done in one hour or less. Of course, you may have even more time to prepare for your next science project or science fair. You can still enjoy this book.

Many experiments are followed by a "Keep Exploring" section. There you will find ideas for projects or experiments. The details are left to you, the young scientist. You will design and carry out your own experiments, **under adult supervision**, when you have more time.

For some experiments, you may need a partner to help you. Work with someone who likes to do experiments as much as you do. Then you will both enjoy what you are doing. **If any safety issues or danger is involved in doing an experiment, you will be warned.** In some cases, to avoid danger, you will be asked to work with an adult. Please do so. Don't take any chances that could lead to an injury.

Desert Biomes

A biome is a region of the earth with a particular climate. A desert biome is one that has a very dry climate. The plants and animals that live in a desert biome are quite similar throughout the world. This book is about desert biomes, but there are other biomes. Earth's biomes include deserts, tundra, taiga, grasslands, rain forests, and temperate forests.

Deserts are regions where there is less than 25 cm (10 in) of rain per year. Most deserts are at latitudes between 15 and 30 degrees north or south of the equator. With so little water in a desert, life is limited. Only plants and animals that can live with very little water are found in a desert biome.

Because it seldom rains in a desert, the air is very dry. The dry air allows nearly all the sun's heat to enter the desert soil. So, daytime temperatures can be very hot. Air temperatures are often 50°C (122°F). Ground temperatures may be as high as 90°C (194°F). At night, the dry air allows heat to escape. The temperature quickly falls and the air can become chilly.

The Gobi Desert is in Mongolia.

The Mojave Desert is in Southern California.

Not all deserts are hot. There are cold deserts such as the Gobi in Mongolia. And there are temperate (mild) deserts. These include the Mojave in Southern California, and the Great Basin east of the Sierra Mountain range in the western United States.

Desert Plants

Most desert plants have many shallow roots that extend outward in all directions. When it does rain, the broad root system can absorb and store much of the water. Some large cactus plants can store as much as 100 liters (27 gallons) of water.

To survive, many desert plants have a short life cycle. When it rains, their seeds quickly germinate, grow, flower, and produce seeds. The seeds then lie dormant until the next rainfall.

Normally, plants lose a lot of water through their leaves. Desert plants are adapted to reduce water loss. Their leaves are tiny or exist as spines or thorns.

Some deserts receive so little rain that nothing can live there. These deserts contain only sand and rocks.

Desert Animals

The top layer of soil in many deserts gets very hot during the day. To escape the heat, many desert animals burrow under the ground. They spend the day resting beneath the upper few centimeters of very hot soil. At night, these animals come out to eat in the cool desert air. Rodents, such as the kangaroo rat, get water from the seeds they eat. Their water losses are small because, unlike you, they have no sweat glands. Desert birds and reptiles feed mostly on insects, which are plentiful. Large desert predators, such as coyotes, hawks, and rattlesnakes, arise after sunset. They eat mostly rodents and rabbits.

The Scientific Method

To do experiments the way scientists do, you need to know about the scientific method.

In most experimenting, scientists make the following steps. They make an observation. They come up with a question. They create a hypothesis (a possible answer to the question). They make a prediction (an if-then statement) based on the hypothesis. They design and do an experiment that will test the prediction. They study the results of the experiment. They form conclusions about their predictions. Then they decide whether the hypothesis is true or false. Scientists share their experimental results by writing articles. The articles are published in science journals.

You might wonder, How do I use the scientific method? You begin when you see, read, or hear about something in the world that makes you curious. So you ask a question. To find an answer, you do a well-designed investigation. You use the scientific method.

Once you have a question, you can make a hypothesis. Your hypothesis is a possible answer to the question (what you think will happen). For example, you might hypothesize that in a hot desert, water will evaporate fast. Once you have a hypothesis, it is time to design an experiment to test your hypothesis.

In most cases, you should do a controlled experiment. This means having two subjects. Both are treated the same except for the one thing being tested. That thing is called a variable. For example, to test the hypothesis above, you might have two identical dishes. You would fill them with water at the same cool temperature. You would place one dish in a very warm room. You would put the other in an identical room at a normal temperature. After several hours, you would measure the volume of water left in each dish. If the volume of water in the warmer room is less than that in the other room, you might conclude that your hypothesis is correct.

The results of one experiment often lead to another question. Or they may send you off in another direction. Whatever the results, something can be learned from every experiment!

Science Fairs

Some of the investigations in this book contain ideas that might be used as a science fair project. Those ideas are indicated with a symbol (🏅) on the Contents page. However, judges at science fairs do not reward projects or experiments that are copied from a book. For example, a diagram of a cactus would not impress most judges. An experiment that measures the percentage of water in desert seeds would be more likely to interest them.

Science fair judges tend to reward creative thought and imagination. It is difficult to be creative or imaginative unless you are really interested in your project. Therefore, try to choose something that excites you. And before you jump into a project, consider your own talents. Consider too the cost of the materials you will need.

If you decide to use an experiment or idea found in this book as a science fair project, find ways to modify or extend it. This should not be difficult. As you carry out investigations, new ideas will come to mind. You will think of questions that experiments can answer. The experiments will make excellent science fair projects. This is especially true when the ideas are yours and are interesting to you.

Safety First

Safety is very important in science. Some of the rules below may seem obvious to you, others may not, but it is important that you follow all of them.

1. Do any experiments or projects **under the adult supervision** of a science teacher or knowledgeable adult.

2. Read all instructions carefully before proceeding with a project. If you have questions, check with your supervisor before going further.

3. **Always wear safety goggles** when doing experiments that could cause particles to enter your eyes. Tie back long hair and do not wear open-toed shoes.

4. Do not eat or drink while experimenting. Never taste substances being used (unless instructed to do so).

5. Do not touch chemicals.

6. Do not let water drops fall on a hot lightbulb.

7. The liquid in some older thermometers is mercury (a dense liquid metal). It is dangerous to touch mercury or breathe its vapor. That is why mercury thermometers have been banned in many states. When doing experiments, use only non-mercury thermometers, such as digital thermometers or those filled with alcohol. If you have a mercury thermometer in the house, **ask an adult** to take it to a place where it can be exchanged or safely discarded.

8. Do only those experiments that are described in the book or those that have been approved by **an adult**.

9. Maintain a serious attitude while conducting experiments. Never engage in horseplay or play practical jokes.

10. Remove all items not needed for the experiment from your work space.

11. At the end of every activity, clean all materials used and put them away. Then wash your hands thoroughly with soap and water.

A Note About Your Notebook

Your notebook, as any scientist will tell you, is a valuable possession. It should contain ideas you may have as you experiment, sketches you draw, calculations you make, and hypotheses you may suggest. It should include a description of every experiment you do. It should include data you record, such as volumes, temperatures, masses, and so on. It should also contain the results of your experiments, graphs you draw, and any conclusions you make based on your results.

30 Minutes or Less

Here are experiments about desert biomes that you can do in 30 minutes or less. If you need to complete a science project by tomorrow, there's not much time left. So let's get started!

1. Using Maps (20 Minutes)

What's the Plan?

Let's find out where desert biomes are located throughout the world. And let's find out in which type of biome you live.

WHAT YOU NEED:

- **map of biomes in Figure 1**
- **map of the world or large world globe**

What You Do

1. Examine the map in Figure 1. It shows where deserts and other biomes are located.

2. Look at the locations of the desert biomes in Figure 1. Compare them with the same locations on a map of the world or on a world globe.

3. On which continents do deserts exist? Are there any continents that do not have desert biomes?

4. Find out where you live on the world map. Use Figure 1 to find the kind of biome where you live.

What's Going On?

You compared the map of biomes in Figure 1 with a map of the world. You could see that deserts are located in North America, South America, Asia, Africa, and Australia. Only Europe has no deserts.

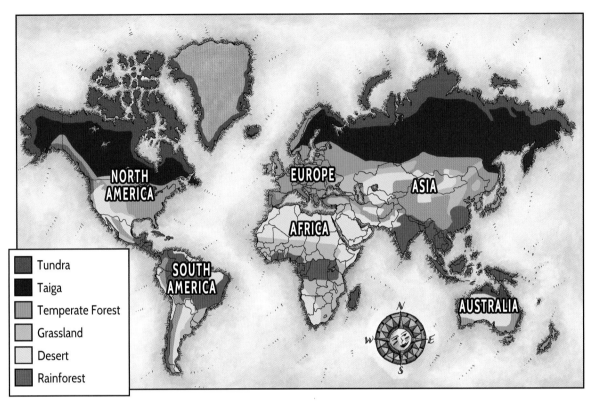

■	Tundra
■	Taiga
▦	Temperate Forest
▦	Grassland
□	Desert
▨	Rainforest

Figure 1. You can see the six land biomes of the world. Which biome do you live in?

By a similar comparison, you could see in which type of biome you live. Don't be surprised if you think the map of biomes for your home is wrong. The map shows what is true for much of the area where you live, not every part of it. For example, the author lives on Cape Cod in Massachusetts. The biome map indicates that he lives in a temperate forest biome. However, the outer end of Cape Cod is covered by sand dunes. Also, while forest covers much of Cape Cod, the trees are shorter than in a typical forest. This is caused by the strong winds and salt air coming off the Atlantic Ocean.

2. A Climatogram of a City in a Desert Biome (20 Minutes)

What's the Plan?

Let's make a climatogram for Riyadh, Saudi Arabia. The climatogram will show the average monthly temperature and rainfall in that city.

> **WHAT YOU NEED:**
> - graph paper or computer
> - pen or pencil
> - Table 1

What You Do

1. Examine Table 1. Use the data in the table to make a climatogram. The climatogram will show the average monthly temperature and rainfall in Riyadh. Figure 2 shows what a sample climatogram looks like. Months of the year are along the horizontal axis. Rainfall is shown on the left vertical axis. Temperatures are shown on the right vertical axis. The average monthly temperature and rainfall for Riyadh is shown in Table 1.

Table 1. Monthly average temperatures and rainfall for Riyadh, Saudi Arabia												
	Jan.	Feb.	Mar.	Apr.	May	Jun.	Jul.	Aug.	Sept.	Oct.	Nov.	Dec.
Temp. (°C)	14.3	16.2	20.8	25.0	30.8	33.6	34.6	34.4	31.4	26.3	20.6	15.4
Rainfall (in.)	0.5	0.4	1.2	1.2	0.5	0.0	0.0	0.0	0.0	0.7	0.2	0.4

2. What is the average temperature for one year in Riyadh?

3. What is the total average rainfall for one year in Riyadh?

4. Is Riyadh dry enough to qualify as part of a desert biome?

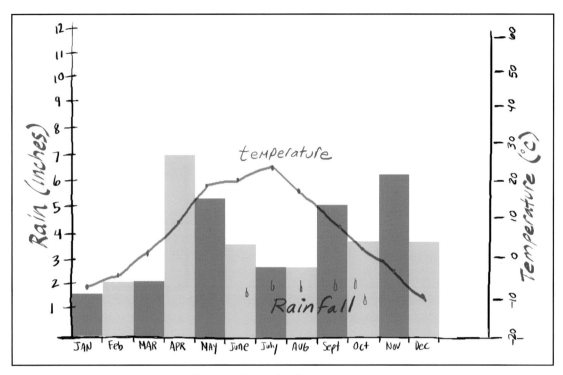

Figure 2. A sample climatogram

What's Going On?

Your climatogram should show Riyadh's average monthly temperature and rainfall. It should be set up like the one in Figure 2. The total rainfall in Riyadh for one year is 5.1 inches. This is less than 10 inches. Therefore, it is part of a desert biome.

Keep Exploring–If You Have More Time!

- Prepare a climatogram of your city or town. Is your total yearly rainfall more than 10 inches?

3. Estivation and Breathing Rate (20 minutes)

What's the Plan?

Desert animals often lower their need for food by estivating. This is similar to hibernating. The animal becomes dormant (inactive). Its breathing and heart rate decrease and its body temperature may fall. The little energy it needs comes from its own body fat. Let's find out how activity affects breathing and heart rates.

What You Do

1. Have a partner lie quietly on a sofa for five minutes. Then measure your partner's heart rate by taking his or her pulse (Figure 3a). You will feel a pulse every time your partner's heart beats. Record the number of pulses you count in 15 seconds. How can you record your partner's heart rate in beats per minute?

2. Measure your partner's breathing rate. To do this, count the number of times his or her abdomen rises in 30 seconds (Figure 3b). Record the breathing rate in breaths per minute.

3. Ask your partner to stand up and run in place for five minutes.

4. After five minutes, quickly take and record your partner's heart rate and breathing rate.

5. How does activity affect a person's heart and breathing rates?

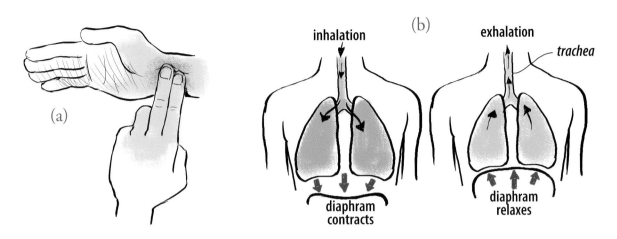

(b)

inhalation

exhalation

trachea

diaphram
contracts

diaphram
relaxes

(a)

Figure 3. a) To feel a pulse, place two fingertips on your partner's lower wrist. b) Your diaphragm contracts when you inhale. It pushes down on your stomach, making your abdomen expand.

What's Going On?

You can measure a heart rate by taking a pulse. Each time the heart beats (contracts), it forces blood into arteries. The arteries expand and create a pulse. You can feel the pulse by touching the artery that passes through a person's wrist. If you take a pulse for 15 seconds, you can multiply the number by 4 to get the heart rate per minute (60 seconds).

Each time a person inhales, the diaphragm contracts. This draws air into the lungs as the contracting diaphragm (Figure 3b) squeezes the abdomen and makes it bulge.

You probably found that heart and breathing rates are lower when a person is resting. When animals estivate, that reduction is much more noticeable.

Keep Exploring–If You Have More Time!

- **Under adult supervision,** measure the heart rate and breathing rate of a pet dog or cat.

- Where else in your body can you feel a pulse?

4. How Desert Snakes Move
(20 minutes)

WHAT YOU NEED:

- **a rug**
- **a linoleum or smooth-tiled floor**

What's the Plan?

Snakes are a common desert reptile. They prey on rodents and other small animals. Snakes have no arms or legs, but they can move. Let's find out how a snake moves.

What You Do

1. Snakes move, but not very fast. The black mamba is probably the fastest snake. It can glide along at about 11 kilometers per hour (7 mph). To see how snakes move, try moving like one. To begin, lie down on a rug.

2. Lie on your side with your legs bent. Lift your shoulders and straighten your legs as you push them against the rug. Your body will move forward.

3. Bend your legs again and repeat the motion. You are moving like a snake, but probably not as fast.

4. Lie on a smooth floor, such as a linoleum or smooth-tiled floor. Try to repeat your snakelike movement. What do you find?

What's Going On?

Snakes move as shown in Figure 4. They have a flexible spine. So snakes can bend their body in an S-shape. Then, using friction, they push against the ground. This makes them move forward. You also use friction to move. When you walk, you push your foot against the ground. The ground pushes back with an equal force. That makes you move forward. If you try to walk on ice, you

Figure 4. Snakes have a flexible spine. They can form waves in their bodies and push forward. This is called serpentine motion. The arrows in the drawing show where the snake's body pushes against the ground.

may slip and fall. There is very little friction between your foot and the ice. You slip when you try to push against smooth ice.

On a rug you were able to move like a snake. But you probably found it difficult to move like a snake on a smooth floor. The smooth floor provided less friction.

Keep Exploring–If You Have More Time!

- Design and do an experiment to show that your foot has to push back in order for you to move forward.

5. Desert Air Currents
(30 minutes)

WHAT YOU NEED:
- **2 clear plastic vials**
- **cold water**
- **food coloring**
- **hot water**
- **eyedropper**

What's the Plan?

Air currents are common in deserts. In fact, desert birds often glide along rising currents of air. Let's find out what causes air currents (upward moving air) in desert biomes.

What You Do

Liquids and gases, such as water and air, are both fluids. That is why liquids and gases behave in similar ways. You can see liquids. But you can't see gases unless they are colored. And air has no color. We can use liquids to explain desert air currents.

1. Nearly fill a clear plastic vial with **cold** water.

2. Add several drops of food coloring to another vial. Then fill it with **hot** water.

3. Use an eyedropper to remove some of the hot colored water.

4. Put the tip of the eyedropper very close to the bottom of the cold water. **Very gently** squeeze the hot water out into the cold water (Figure 5). What happens? How does this experiment help you understand desert air currents?

Figure 5. Very gently squeeze the hot colored water under the clear, cold water. What happens?

20

What's Going On?

You saw the hot water move up in cold water. Hot water is less dense than cold water. This means hot water weighs less than an equal volume of cold water. You know that less dense things, such as wood, float on more dense things, such as water. Similarly, hot air will float on cold air. The sun heats desert soil to temperatures as high as 90°C (194°F). The air near the hot ground becomes warmer than nearby cooler air. Like the hot water in your experiment, the hot air is less dense than nearby cooler air. So the cooler air moves under the hotter air. This creates an upward current of air.

Birds can catch upward air currents rising from the desert.

Keep Exploring–If You Have More Time!

* Repeat Experiment 5, but this time add colored cold water to hot water. Try to predict what will happen.

* Design and do an experiment to show that warm air rises in a heated room.

One Hour or Less

Is there only an hour left to prepare a science project? Here are experiments that meet your need.

6. Which Gets Hotter: Water or Desert Soil?
(1 hour)

What's the Plan?

Most desert soil is very dry and sandy. Let's see how this affects the temperature of desert soil.

What You Do

1. Add 100 grams of water at room temperature to a clear plastic cup or drinking glass. Add an equal mass of dry sand at room temperature to an identical cup or glass.

2. Place both the sand and the water under a heat lamp or under a hot summer sun (Figure 6). Be sure both sand and water receive the same amount of light.

3. Wait for the water temperature to rise about 10 °C (18 °F).

4. Remove both the sand and water from the source of heat.

WHAT YOU NEED:

- water
- 2 clear plastic cups or drinking glasses
- balance for weighing to ±1 gram
- dry sand
- 1 or 2 thermometers (−10 to 50°C or 0 to 120°F)
- heat lamp or hot summer sun
- pen or pencil
- notebook

22

5. Stir both sand and water and record their final temperatures. In which substance (sand or water) was the increase in temperature greater?

6. How would rain affect the temperature of desert soil?

Figure 6. Which gets hotter, sand or water?

What's Going On?

You probably found the sand temperature increased more than the water temperature. Suppose you have equal masses (grams) of sand and water. To raise the water temperature one degree requires more heat than to raise the sand temperature one degree. Under a blazing sun, the temperature of desert soil can reach 90°C (194°F). Under the same sun, the temperature of a lake or pond would be much lower.

Keep Exploring—If You Have More Time!

- Do an experiment to find out how a soil's color affects its absorption of heat from the sun.

- Suppose you add the same amount of heat to equal masses of water and cooking oil at room temperature. In which liquid would the temperature increase more?

23

7. The Kit Fox: Adapted for Hearing
(1 hour)

What's the Plan?

The photograph to the right shows a desert animal—a kit fox. Its scientific name is *Vulpes macrotis*. Its cute face resembles that of a corgi (a breed of dog). It is the smallest of what biologists call the Canidae family. That family includes dogs, wolves, coyotes, and foxes. One of the kit fox's outstanding features are its very large ears. A kit fox's ears vary in length from 7 to 9.5 cm (2.8 to 3.8 in). Its body length is only 45 to 53 cm (18 to 21 in). So its ears are about one-fifth as long as its body.

Kit foxes are usually gray with rust-colored tones. Their bellies are white. In the winter, their coats become silvery. Their tails are about 30 cm (12 in) long with a black tip.

Like many desert animals, kit foxes are nocturnal. They leave their dens after sunset to hunt. Their diet includes kangaroo rats, rabbits, voles, prairie dogs, snakes, lizards, insects, and ground birds. Occasionally, they eat carrion or cactus fruits when their favorite foods are not available. As part of a food chain, kit foxes are the prey of coyotes.

Unlike a dog, the hair between a kit fox's foot pads is very thick. The hair provides good traction as the foxes run on sandy soil. They can run at a speed of 40 kilometers per hour (25 mph). The thick hair helps to insulate their feet from the hot desert soil.

Kit foxes live in the deserts of southwestern United States and northern Mexico. They have a life span of up to seven years. They mate in late December and early January. After a gestation period of approximately nine weeks, the

> **WHAT YOU NEED:**
> - ruler or measuring tape
> - a partner
> - pen or pencil
> - notebook

A kit fox's ears are large to help it give off heat during the hot days in the desert.

Kit foxes live in burrows in the desert. They come out at night when it is cool.

females have litters of one to seven pups. The pups are weaned after four months and become independent after five or six months.

Kit foxes live in dens. Their dens are often made by modifying the burrows of other animals. Sometimes they live in culverts or large abandoned pipes. Or they may dig burrows in banks of soil.

Let's find out what advantage is provided by the kit fox's large ears.

What You Do

1. A kit fox's ear is about one-fifth (20 percent) as long as its body. To give you an idea of what this means, measure the length of someone's ear. Then measure the length of that person's torso. Measure from top of shoulder to top of leg. What percentage of the person's body length is his or her ear? Suppose the person's ear were 20 percent of his or her height? How long would it be?

2. The kit fox's large ears allow it to hear very well. This is a valuable asset in detecting its next meal or in eluding a coyote. To see why ear size helps hearing, increase the size of your own ears. You can do this by cupping your hands behind your ears. What sounds can you hear now that you couldn't when your "ears" were smaller?

What's Going On?

By cupping your hands around your ears, you increased the surface area of your ears. The larger surface area reflected more sound into your ears. You probably heard sounds of a low intensity that you had not heard before.

8. The Kit Fox: Adapted for Staying Cool in a Desert (1 hour)

What's the Plan?

If you did Experiment 7, you know that a kit fox has huge ears. Let's find out how those large ears help the animal lose heat and stay cool.

What You Do

A kit fox's ears expose a lot of surface to the air. Let's see how a large surface area helps the body lose heat.

1. Add 500 mL (2 cups) of very hot water to a large measuring cup. Pour half the water into a wide, shallow dish. Pour the other 250 mL into a narrower cylinder or drinking glass (Figure 7). In which container does the water have more surface exposed to the cooler air?

2. Measure the initial (starting) temperature of the water in each container. Then measure the temperature in each container every five minutes.

WHAT YOU NEED:

- **very hot water**
- **measuring cup**
- **wide, shallow, plastic dish and a narrower cylinder or drinking glass**
- **one or two laboratory thermometers to measure water temperature**
- **clock or watch**
- **pen or pencil**
- **notebook**

28

3. Continue to measure temperatures for at least 40 minutes. In which container does the water lose heat faster?

Figure 7. How does surface area affect the rate at which things lose heat and cool?

What's Going On?

The larger surface area exposed more water to the cooler air, so it lost heat faster. In the same way, the large surface area of the kit fox's ears allows it to lose heat faster. Its ears help keep it cool. If its ears were smaller, it would not be able to lose heat as fast. With smaller ears, it would not be able to survive in a hot desert.

Keep Exploring—If You Have More Time!

- How does body size affect surface area and the ability to lose heat? To find out, make some cubes from clay. Make one that is one centimeter on a side. Make one that is two centimeters on a side. Make one that is four centimeters on a side.

- For each cube you made, divide its surface area by its volume. Does its surface area increase as fast as its volume?

- Explain why parents must keep babies warmer than older and bigger children.

9. How Surface Area Affects Water Loss (1 hour)

What's the Plan?

Plants lose water through their leaves. Most desert plants have very small leaves or modified leaves (spines or thorns). The surface area of these leaves, thorns, or spines is very small. Let's find out how the small surface area of a desert plant's leaves helps it survive in a hot dry climate.

WHAT YOU NEED:

- paper towels
- sink
- cold water faucet
- balance that can weigh to ±1 gram
- string or clothesline
- clothespins
- clock or watch
- pen or pencil
- notebook

What You Do

1. Hold two folded paper towels in a sink under a cold water faucet.

2. Open the towels. Let any excess water drain away into the sink.

3. Fold both towels and weigh them on a balance that can weigh to ±1 gram. Record the weight of each towel in your notebook.

4. Fully open one towel. Hang it on a string or clothesline.

5. Fold the other towel into a small square. Hang it on the same line.

6. After about one hour, reweigh each towel. From which towel did more water evaporate?

What's Going On?

You probably found that more water evaporated from the open towel. It had more surface area exposed to the air than the folded towel. Desert plants conserve water. They do so by having leaves with small surface areas. Or they have modified leaves (spines and thorns). With less leaf surface exposed to the air, less water evaporates from the plants.

Keep Exploring—If You Have More Time!

- Which solid shape—cylinder, sphere, cone, cube, or parallelepiped—has the least surface area per volume?

Most desert plants have small leaves or modified leaves, such as the spines on this cactus.

10. How Temperature Keeps a Desert Dry
(1 hour)

What's the Plan?

Most desert plants and animals live in a very warm environment. Let's find out why high temperatures keep a desert very dry.

What You Do

1. Wet two folded paper towels in a sink. Hold them under a running cold water faucet.

2. Open the towels. Let any excess water drain away into the sink.

3. Fold both towels. Then weigh them on a balance that can weigh to ±1 gram. Record the weight of each towel in your notebook.

4. Fully open both towels. Hang one on a line in a cool room.

5. Hang the other towel as shown in Figure 8. It will be in the warm air coming from an oven set at 200°F.

6. After one hour, reweigh each towel and record its weight. From which towel did more water evaporate?

WHAT YOU NEED:
- paper towels
- sink
- cold water
- faucet
- balance that can weigh to ±1 gram
- clothesline or string
- clothespins
- oven
- weight
- clock or watch
- pen or pencil
- notebook

What's Going On?

You probably found that more water evaporated from the towel that was in warm air. Desert heat causes water to evaporate rapidly. That is why soil, plants, and everything else dries quickly in a desert.

Keep Exploring—If You Have More Time!

- Design an experiment to show that evaporation has a cooling effect.

Figure 8. Does temperature affect the rate at which water evaporates?

11. How Desert Bats Find Their Food (1 hour)

Bats use echolocation to hunt at night.

What's the Plan?

Like most desert mammals, bats are active at night. They spend their days hanging in caves. Emerging at night, they feed on insects, which they catch in flight. Bats have eyes, but they can't see their prey in the dark. Even so, they fly through darkness, swerving about solid objects as if it were daytime. They use sound, not light, to "see" at night. Their secret is echolocation. They emit sound waves with frequencies as high as 100,000 vibrations per second. Hearing the reflected echoes of these sounds enables them to detect objects in their path. Humans can't hear these high-pitched sounds. We are limited to sound frequencies between 20 and 20,000 vibrations per second. And as we age, our ability to sense high frequencies decreases.

At frequencies near 100,000 vibrations per second, sound waves are only millimeters apart. This allows flying bats to detect and locate the small insects on which they feed.

Now let's do an experiment to see how sound waves are reflected.

What You Do

You know that light can be reflected. Just look in a mirror. You see the reflected light coming from your face. The angle at which a light ray strikes a mirror always equals the angle at which it is reflected. Figure 9a shows a light ray traveling to and from a mirror. You can see that angle i, the angle of incidence, equals angle r, the angle of reflection. You can check on this for yourself. Do an experiment like the one shown in Figure 9b. Do it in a dark room.

Now let's see if sound is reflected in the same way as light.

1. Find two long cardboard tubes. You also need an object that produces a sound of low intensity. A ticking wristwatch works well. You'll also need a partner to help you.

2. Have your partner hold the watch at one end of a tube. The other end of that tube should be near a smooth concrete wall in a quiet area. A basement or empty classroom wall works well.

3. Have your partner turn the tube so that it makes an angle with the wall as shown in Figure 9c.

a)

Figure 9. a) Light is reflected at the same angle (r) in which it hits the mirror (i).

35

b)

black paper mask

same light ray reflected

slit

Figure 9. b) You can do an experiment to show that angle *i* equals angle *r*.

c)

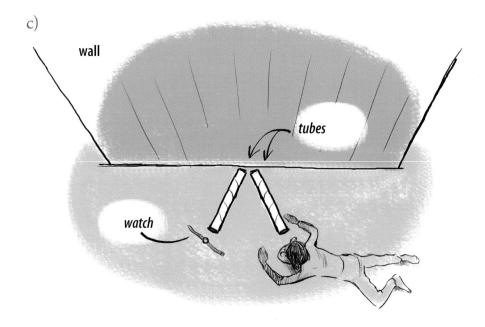

wall

tubes

watch

Figure 9. c) Does sound reflect in the same way as light?

4. Hold your ear against one end of the second tube. Place the other end of the tube near the end of the tube that your friend is holding.

5. Slowly change the angle that your tube makes with the wall. Stop when you hear the faint ticking sound most clearly and loudly. Then compare the angle that each tube makes with the wall.

6. Repeat the experiment several times. Each time have your partner change the angle that his tube makes with the wall. After each angle change, compare the angles the two tubes make with the wall when you can best hear the sound. What can you conclude about the reflection of sound?

7. Hold the spout (the narrow end) of a large plastic funnel next to your ear. If you can't find a funnel, roll several sheets of paper into a cone open at both ends. Place the narrow end of the cone next to your ear. Turn the funnel or cone toward a source of sound. What happens to the intensity (loudness) of the sound? What happens when you remove the funnel? Why do you think the funnel can increase the intensity of a sound?

What's Going On?

You probably found the ticking was loudest when the two tubes made the same angle with the wall. That shows sound is reflected in the same way as light. Angle i equals angle r for sound just as it does for light.

The large funnel reflected more sound than usual into your ear. That increased the intensity of the sounds you heard.

Keep Exploring—If You Have More Time!

- Before hearing aids were invented, people who were hearing impaired often used ear trumpets. What were ear trumpets and how did they help people hear better?

More Than One Hour

Here are experiments for the budding scientist who has more time for a science project! It will be time well spent.

12. How Much Water Is There in Seeds and Foods? (2 hours)

What's the Plan?

Many small desert animals get their water from seeds and other food they eat. Do seeds and foods really contain water? Let's find out.

What You Do

1. Find some cylindrical aluminum pans about 8 cm (3 in) in diameter.

2. Weigh one of the pans on a balance. Then add about 30 grams of one kind of seed. Record the weight of the seeds plus the pan.

3. Weigh other seeds and pieces of foods. You might weigh seeds of pinto beans, lima beans, green beans, acorns (from oak trees in the fall), winter rye, or other seeds, as well as pieces of an apple, banana, carrot, broccoli, etc.

4. Place the small pans on a large pan. Then **ask an adult** to put the large pan in an oven at 300°F for one hour. Heat is a drying agent. It will remove some or all of the water that may be in the seeds or foods.

> **WHAT YOU NEED:**
> - **an adult**
> - **cylindrical aluminum pans about 8 cm (3 in) in diameter**
> - **balance**
> - **seeds and foods**
> - **pen or pencil**
> - **notebook**
> - **oven mitts**
> - **oven**
> - **insulated pads**
> - **large pan**

5. After an hour, ask the adult, wearing oven mitts, to remove the pan from the oven. It can be placed on insulated pads. Let the seeds and foods cool.

6. When they have cooled, reweigh the pans with the seeds or food. Record the weights and any weight lost. What do you conclude? Was there water in the seeds and foods? If all the water present was removed, what percentage of the original weight of each food or seed was water?

What's Going On?

You probably found that all the seeds and foods lost weight. That proves there was water in the foods. The percentage of water was probably greater in foods than in seeds.

Do you think bean seeds contain water? One of these seeds has germinated.

39

13. Temperatures on and Under the Ground (1 day)

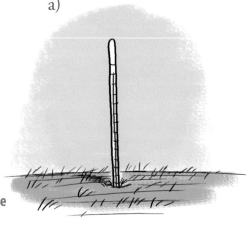

WHAT YOU NEED:

- **laboratory or household thermometer**
- **very long spike or a strong pointed stick**
- **spade**
- **pen or pencil**
- **notebook**
- **grass or yard**
- **watch or clock**

What's the Plan?

Let's find out why so many desert animals spend the day underground.

What You Do

1. On a warm sunny morning, place a thermometer on some grass. Cover the thermometer bulb with grass or leaves. It should not be exposed to the sun's direct rays. After about five minutes, or when the temperature remains constant, read and record the temperature.

2. If you are using a laboratory thermometer, use a very long spike or a strong pointed stick to make a deep, narrow hole in the soft ground. Insert the thermometer into the hole (Figure 10a). If you are using a household thermometer, use a shovel or spade to make a deep cut in the soil. Insert the thermometer into the slit (Figure 10b). Replace the sod. After five minutes, measure and record the temperature under the ground.

a)

Figure 10. a) Measure temperatures above and under the ground.

40

3. Repeat these measurements every one or two hours throughout the day.

4. Can you make any conclusions about temperatures on and below the ground?

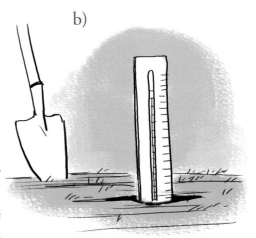

What's Going On?

You probably found that the temperature on the ground increased until mid-afternoon and then began to fall. The underground temperature probably remained fairly constant throughout the day.

Figure 10. b) For a household thermometer, use a shovel to make a deep slit in the ground.

In a desert, daytime underground temperatures are much lower than temperatures on the sun-heated soil. That is why so many desert animals retreat to underground burrows during the daytime.

Keep Exploring—If You Have More Time!

* Repeat this experiment at different times of the year. What differences do you find?

14. Soil Types, Moisture, and Seed Germination (1 week)

What's the Plan?

Let's compare seed germination in desert soil and ordinary garden soil.

What You Do

1. Add dry sand to an aluminum pie pan until it is about an inch deep.

2. Add an equal amount of moist garden soil to an identical pie pan.

3. To the soil in each pan add a dozen radish seeds or winter rye seeds. Space the seeds approximately equal distances apart.

4. Cover the seeds on the dry sand with about an inch more of dry sand. Cover the seeds on garden soil with about an inch more of garden soil.

5. Keep the garden soil moist but not wet.

6. After several days, begin looking for small seedlings. Have any seeds germinated? Do you find seedlings in the desert soil? In the garden soil?

What's Going On?

You probably found that the seeds in the garden soil germinated after several days and their leaves appeared above the soil. It is unlikely that seeds in desert

WHAT YOU NEED:

- very dry sand
- 2 aluminum pie pans
- moist garden soil
- 2 dozen radish seeds or winter rye seeds
- water

soil will germinate. Water is needed for seeds to germinate. Because desert soil is very dry, seeds there will not germinate unless it rains.

Spring rain often causes the desert in southern California to bloom. This happens when dormant seeds receive the water they need to germinate. A desert in bloom attracts tourists and natives alike.

Keep Exploring—If You Have More Time!

* Simulate a desert rainstorm by adding water to the dry sand until it is saturated. Will the seeds now germinate as they would if they were desert plants?

A desert blooms after the rain.

15. How Does Your Rainfall Compare with Desert Rainfall?

(1 month or more)

What's the Plan?

To measure rainfall, you need a rain gauge. Then you can compare your rainfall with that found in deserts.

What You Do

Rain is measured by the depth of the water it produces.

1. If you don't have a rain gauge, you can make one. Find a clear glass or plastic jar with straight sides. An olive jar works well.

2. Place the jar in an open area away from buildings and trees. You might tape the jar to a stake. Or you could **ask an adult** to drill a shallow hole slightly larger than the jar's diameter in the top of a post. The jar could be set in the opening.

3. After a rainfall, measure the depth of the water in the jar with a ruler. Another option is to tape a clear ruler or ruled tape to the side of the jar. Or you might put a strip of tape on the side of the jar. You could then mark a scale on the tape with lines 0.5 cm (1/4 in) apart (Figure 11).

WHAT YOU NEED:

- **clear glass or plastic jar with straight sides such as an olive jar**
- **an adult**
- **stake or post**
- **sturdy tape**
- **ruler, clear ruler, or ruled tape**
- **pen or pencil**
- **notebook**
- **local newspaper**

4. After measuring a rainfall, record your measurement, empty the jar, and replace it. You might compare your measurement of rainfall with one found in your local newspaper.

5. Measure the total rainfall for at least one month. Record the rainfall each time it rains. At the end of the month, add your numbers to find the total for the month.

Deserts have less than 25 cm (10 in) of rain per year. The average monthly rainfall would be about 2 cm (7/8 in). How does your rainfall compare with that of a desert? Of course, a better way to compare would be to record rainfall for more than one month.

What's Going On?

Unless you live in a desert, you probably found your rainfall exceeded 25 cm (10 in) per year. However, during a drought, your rainfall might be similar to that of a desert.

Keep Exploring–If You Have More Time!

Snow can be measured as rainfall, but an inch of snow usually contains much less water than an inch of rain. Find a way to convert the depth of a snowfall to centimeters or inches of rain. But remember, two feet of light fluffy snow might equal an inch of rain. However, 3 or 4 inches of wet slushy snow might provide an inch of rain.

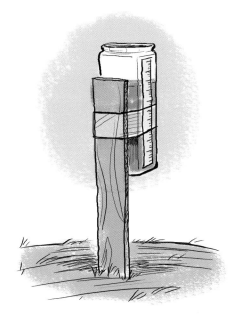

Figure 11. You can make a rain gauge to measure rainfall.

Words to Know

biome—A region of the earth with a characteristic climate and species of plants and animals.

breathing rate—The number of breaths taken per minute.

climatogram—A graph that shows annual monthly rainfall and temperature for a particular place on the earth, such as a city or town.

desert—A biome characterized by a dry climate with less than 25 cm (10 in) of rain per year.

echolocation—A method used by some animals, such as bats, to locate objects.

estivation—A state similar to hibernation in which an animal becomes dormant. Its heart and breathing rates decrease and its energy requirements are greatly reduced.

evaporation—The change of a liquid to a gas.

germination—The emergence of a baby plant from a seed.

heart rate—The number of times the heart beats per minute.

hibernation—A state in which an animal's activity and bodily functions are greatly reduced so that its need for food is minimal or nonexistent.

latitude—A location north or south of the equator. Latitude is measured in degrees. The equator is defined as latitude 0 degrees; the Poles are 90 degrees north and south of the equator. A degree of latitude along the earth's surface is approximately 111 km (69 mi).

Further Reading

Books

Bardhan-Quallen, Sudipta. *Championship Science Fair Projects: 100 Sure-to-Win Experiments*. New York: Sterling, 2007.

Benoit, Peter. *Deserts*. New York: Children's Press, 2011.

Ceceri, Kathryn, and Sam Carbaugh. *Discover the Desert: The Driest Place on Earth*. White River Junction, Vt.: Nomad Press, 2009.

Latham, Donna. *Amazing Biome Projects You Can Build Yourself*. White River Junction, Vt.: Nomad Press, 2009.

Pyers, Greg. *Biodiversity of Deserts*. New York: Marshall Cavendish Benchmark, 2010.

Rhatigan, Joe, and Rain Newcomb. *Prize-Winning Science Fair Projects for Curious Kids*. New York: Lark Books, 2006.

Web Sites

Desert Biome
<http://www.kidcyber.com.au/topics/biomedesert.htm>

Kids Do Ecology: Desert
<http://kids.nceas.ucsb.edu/biomes/desert.html>

Index

5